The Emperor Julian's Oration to

the Mother of the Gods

Emperor Julian

Kessinger Publishing's Rare Reprints

Thousands of Scarce and Hard-to-Find Books
on These and other Subjects!

- Americana
- Ancient Mysteries
- Animals
- Anthropology
- Architecture
- Arts
- Astrology
- Bibliographies
- Biographies & Memoirs
- Body, Mind & Spirit
- Business & Investing
- Children & Young Adult
- Collectibles
- Comparative Religions
- Crafts & Hobbies
- Earth Sciences
- Education
- Ephemera
- Fiction
- Folklore
- Geography
- Health & Diet
- History
- Hobbies & Leisure
- Humor
- Illustrated Books
- Language & Culture
- Law
- Life Sciences

- Literature
- Medicine & Pharmacy
- Metaphysical
- Music
- Mystery & Crime
- Mythology
- Natural History
- Outdoor & Nature
- Philosophy
- Poetry
- Political Science
- Science
- Psychiatry & Psychology
- Reference
- Religion & Spiritualism
- Rhetoric
- Sacred Books
- Science Fiction
- Science & Technology
- Self-Help
- Social Sciences
- Symbolism
- Theatre & Drama
- Theology
- Travel & Explorations
- War & Military
- Women
- Yoga
- *Plus Much More!*

We kindly invite you to view our catalog list at:
http://www.kessinger.net

The

EMPEROR JULIAN'S
ORATION
to the
MOTHER OF THE GODS

✢

IS it therefore requisite that we should speak
about particulars of this kind; and that we
should divulge, by a written oration, things
which it is not lawful to mention, and which
are ineffable? I mean, who Attis or Gallus
is; and who the mother of the gods: what the
particulars are respecting her sacred rites;
and on what account they were delivered to
us at first: for they were delivered indeed by
the most antient Phrygians, and were first
of all received by the Greeks, not indeed in-
discriminately, but by the Athenians, after

I 2

they had learned by experience that they were very far from acting properly in deriding him who performed the orgies of the mother of the gods. For they report that Gallus was injuriously treated, and ejected by the Athenians as one who introduced novelties in divine concerns; and this because they did not as yet understand the properties of the goddess, and her agreement with Deo, Rhea, and Ceres. But this injurious conduct was followed by the avenging anger of the god, and an expiation of his wrath. For the priest of the Pythian god, who becomes the leader of the Greeks in all their illustrious under-takings, exhorted them to appease the anger of the mother of the gods; in consequence of which, as they report, a temple was raised to the goddess, in which all the public writings of the Athenians are preserved.

But after the Greeks, the Romans received the same sacred rites, the Pythian deity per-suading them also to this undertaking, that they might procure the presence of the Phry-gian goddess as a military associate in the Carthaginian war. And here perhaps it will not be improper to insert the following short history of this affair. As soon as the Romans had received the oracle of Apollo, the inhabitants of Rome, the friend of divinity, sent an ambassador to the kings of Pergamus, who then reigned in Phrygia, and ordered him to request of the Phrygians the most holy image of the goddess: but the ambassador receiving the sacred burthen, placed it in a good-sailing vessel, and which was in every respect well adapted to swim over such a length of sea. The ship therefore, having passed over the Ægean and Ionian, and sailed about the Sicilian and Tyrrhene sea, drove at length to the mouth of the Tyber. But then the common people of Rome, together with the senate, poured forth to the spectacle: and the priests and priestesses in particular were far more eager on this occasion than the rest; all of whom, invested with becoming ornaments, and such as were agreeable to the custom of their country, attentively fixed their eyes on the ship sailing with a prosperous course, and on the impetuosity of the parted billows as they dashed about the keel. But afterwards, when the ship drove into the port, each person adored the statue at a distance from the place where he happened to stand. But the goddess, as if willing to convince the Roman people that they had not led from Phrygia an inanimate image, but something endued with a greater and more divine power than ordinary*, stopped the vessel as soon as it reached the Tyber, and suddenly rooted it, as it were, in the stream. Hence, on the people endeavouring to draw it against the tide, it resisted their efforts, and remained fixed; nor did it in the least yield to their attempts of thrusting it forward; and though every artifice was employed for this purpose, yet it still remained immovable. In consequence of this, a dire and unjust sus-

---

*To believe that the statues of the gods, such as they were fabricated by the ancients, participated of a divine influence, as much as the substances from which they were composed is capable of admitting, must appear ridiculous to every one who is ignorant that the construction of these statues was the result of the most consummate theological science, and that from their apt resemblance to divine natures they became participants of divine illumination. For, as Sallust well observes, in his treatise *On the Gods and the World,* (chap. 15) "As the providence of the gods is every where extended, a certain habitude or fitness is all that is requisite in order to receive their beneficent communications. But all habitude is produced through imitation and similitude; and hence temples imitate the heavens, but altars the earth; *statues resemble life, and on this account they are similar to animals;* and prayers imitate that which is intellectual; but characters, superior ineffable powers; herbs and stones resemble matter; and animals which are sacrificed the irrational life of our souls." Statues therefore, through their habitude or fitness, conjoin the souls of those who pray to them with the gods themselves: and when we view the ancient mode of worshiping images in this light, we shall find it equally as rational as any other mode of conduct in which a certain end is proposed to be obtained by *legitimate* means.

picion arose against the all-sacred priesthood of the consecrated virgin; and Clodia (for this was the name of the venerable virgin) was accused as one not perfectly pure, and who had not preserved herself inviolate to the goddess; and hence it was said, the divinity gave evident tokens of indignation and wrath; for it now appeared to every one that the image was something more divine than usual.

But in consequence of this suspicion, the

Some of these statues were called *Diopeteis,* or *such as descended from heaven,* "because, (says Jamblichus apud Phot. p. 554) the occult art by which they were fabricated by human hands was inconspicuous." And we are informed by Proclus on Euclid, in his comment on the definition of *Figure,* "that this occult or theurgic art fashioned some of the resemblances of the gods, by characters, in an ineffable manner; for characters of this kind manifest the unknown powers of the gods: but others it imitated by forms and images; fashioning some of them erect and others sitting; and some similar to a heart, but others spherical; and others it expressed by different figures. And, again, some it fabricated of a simple form, but others it composed from a multitude of forms; and some of these were sacred and venerable, but others domestic, exhibiting the peculiar gentleness of the gods: and some it constructed of a severe aspect; and lastly, attributed to others different symbols, according to the similitude and sympathy pertaining to the gods." Let not the reader, however, confound this *scientific worship* of the ancients with the *filthy piety,* as Proclus in his hymn to the Muses justly calls it, of the Catholics: for it is surely one thing to worship the images of those *giant-like Barbarians* called *Saints,* and another to reverence the *resemblances of divinity;* since the former conduct is *horridly impious and full of delusion and insanity;* but the latter is *beautifully pious,* is *replete* with *real good,* and is *divinely wise.*

virgin was at first filled with shame, so very
remote was she from a conduct so unlawful
and base. But when she perceived that the
accusation against her gathered strength,
then, unbinding her zone, and girding it
round the extremity of the ship, like one agitated by divine inspiration, she ordered all
the multitude to depart. Afterwards she en-
treated the goddess that she would not suffer
her to be circumvented by unjust blas-
phemies: and then, as they report, raising
her voice, as if she was giving a nautical signal, *O, queen mother,* (says she) *if I am
chaste, follow me.* But after she had thus
spoken, she not only moved the ship, but drew
it for a considerable space along the stream.
And these two circumstances the goddess exhibited to the Romans for the purpose, as it
appears to me, of convincing them that they
had not brought from Phrygia a burthen of
inconsiderable honour, but one worthy the
highest estimation, as not being any thing
human but truly divine; nor a piece of inanimate earth, but an inspired and divine possession. This then was one of the particulars
which the goddess exhibited to the Romans;
but the other, that no citizen, whether virtu-
ous or depraved, could be concealed from her

inspection. And besides this, the Romans from that time warred on the Carthaginians with prosperous success.

These historical particulars therefore, though they may appear incredible to some, and neither adapted to a philosopher nor a theologist, ought, nevertheless, to be mentioned; for they are commonly related by most historians, and the representation of them is yet preserved in brazen images in Rome, the most powerful of cities, and beloved by the gods. Though I am not ignorant that some of *the vehemently wise* will consider these matters as the intolerable trifles of old women; but to me it appears more proper to give credit to cities in these affairs, than to such *knowing* men, whose *little* soul is indeed acute, but beholds nothing with a vision healthy and sound.

But I hear that Porphyry has philosophized about some of those particulars which I had an intention of discoursing upon during the time in which the sacred rites of the goddess were celebrated; but I know not what Porphyry has said on this occasion, nor have I yet met with his discourse on the subject, though it may happen that his opinion may

K

be coincident wih mine. But I (as the result of my own spontaneous conceptions on the occasion) understand by Gallus and Attis, the essence of that prolific and demiurgic intellect which generates all things even to the lowest matter, and which contains in itself all the reasons and causes of material forms: for the forms of all things do not subsist in all, nor are the ideas of the lowest and last of things, which possess nothing but the name of privation, with an obscure conception, in the most supreme and first of causes*. As therefore there are many essences, and many artificers of things, that nature of the third demiurgus, (who contains the exempt reasons, and continued causes, of material forms), which, descending from on high, through the stars, pervades through prolific abundance as far as to the earth, is that Attis

---

*I have already observed, in the Introduction to this volume, that our religious Emperor had not arrived at the most consummate degree of perfection in philosophic attainments, and the present passage proves the truth of my assertion; for, in reality, the lowest forms subsist in the highest, and the highest in the lowest; but with this difference, that the lowest are contained in the highest in a paradigmatical or causal manner, and the highest in the lowest according to ultimate subjection, or after the manner of images. So that all forms subsist in each, but in a manner accommodated to the nature of each; just as earth subsists in heaven *celestially,* and heaven in earth according to a *terrestrial property.*

who is the subject of our present investigation. But perhaps it is necessary to express my meaning more clearly.

We say then, that matter is something, and that there is also a material form; but unless we admit that there is a certain cause which has an establishment prior to these, we shall, through ignorance, verge to an Epicurean opinion: for if there be nothing more ancient than these two principles, the realms of generation must be alloted a rash and fortuitous impulse. But we may perceive (says a certain sagacious Peripatetic, such as Xenarchus) that the cause of these is a fifth and circular body*. But it appears to me that both Aristotle and Theophrastus are ridiculously anxious about a body of this kind, and that they are ignorant, as it were, of their own voice. For, as when we have arrived at an incorporeal and intelligible essence it is necessary to stop, and not to investigate any superior cause, but content ourselves with saying, that these things are thus naturally established, so, (say they) with respect to the fifth body, it is necessary to acknowledge

---

*Concerning this fifth body, see my Introduction to the Timæus of Plato.

K 2

that it naturally subsists in this manner; to
explore no other causes, but to stop here,
without ascending to an intelligible essence,
which, as it is naturally in itself nothing, so
it is nothing but an empty conception in the
soul; for after this manner I remember to
have heard Xenarchus discoursing; but
whether he is right or not in such assertions,
I shall leave to the first-rate Peripatetics to
determine. That this, indeed, is not agreeable to my opinions on the subject, must be
perfectly evident to every one; since I consider the hypotheses of Aristotle as wanting
support, unless they are conciliated with
those of Plato; or rather unless they are
found to be consonant to the oracles of the
gods.

But perhaps it is worth inquiring how a
circular body is capable of containing the
causes of material forms, for it is manifest
and clear, that without these, generation cannot possibly subsist: for on what account are
so many things generated? From whence do
the male and female natures originate? From
whence the difference of things subsisting according to genus in bounded forms, unless
there are certain previously-subsisting and
presiding reasons and causes which pre-exist

as paradigms, and to the perception of which, if our sight is dull, we should still farther purify the eyes of our soul? But proper purgation consists in a conversion of the soul to itself, and a perception how soul and a material intellect are, as it were, certain express resemblances and images of immaterial* forms: for there is not any one body, or any thing incorporeal, which subsists and is beheld about bodies, the image of which intellect is not able to receive in an incorporeal manner; and this it could never be able to accomplish unless it possessed something naturally allied to these. On this account Aristotle also says, that the soul is the place of forms, not indeed in energy, but in capacity only†. It is necessary therefore that such a soul, and which converts itself to the body, should possess these in capacity: and if there is any soul unrestrained by, and unmixed with, the body, we ought to think that all things subsist in such a soul no longer in capacity but in perfect energy.

---

*The original is ενυλων, but should doubtless be αυλων.

†The soul is, indeed παμμορφον αγαλμα, an *omniform image;* and the forms which partial souls like ours contain, are, prior to the illuminations of science, said to be in capacity, because they are then in a dormant state, and may be compared to beautiful colours secluded from the light.

But we shall understand this more clearly by means of the paradigm which Plato employs in the Sophista, though for a purpose different from the present. But I do not introduce this example with a view to give demonstration to what has been said, for it is not proper to receive this by demonstration, but by a *direct application of intellect** alone: for our discourse is about first principles, or things co-ordinate with such as are first; since Attis is considered by us, and with great propriety, as a god. But what, and of what kind, is this example? Plato then says, that, among those who are conversant with imitation, if any one wishes to imitate in such a manner as to emulate the real subsistence of the things imitated, such an undertaking will be laborious and difficult, and almost next to impossible; but that the imitation of things according to their appearance is easy, expeditious, and extremely possible. When, therefore, receiving a mir-

---

*The νοερα επιβολη, or *application of intellect,* which the Emperor mentions in this place, signifies that *self-inspective* power of intellect by which it is able to pass into immediate contact with ideas superior to such as are participated by soul: and a knowledge of this kind is superior to that of science, above which it is immediately situated. See more concerning this in a note to my translation of the Phædo of Plato.

ror, we carry it about, we may easily exhibit the representations of the several species of things. Let us now transfer the similitude of this example to the subject of our investigation; and let the mirror be that which is called by Aristotle the place in capacity of forms: but it is perfectly necessary that the forms themselves should subsist in energy prior to capacity. Since our soul therefore contains, as it appears to Aristotle, the forms of things in capacity, where shall we first place these as subsisting in energy? Shall we establish them in material natures? But these are evidently the last of things. It remains, therefore, that we should explore immaterial causes, which subsist in energy prior to material natures, and from which, having a prior subsistence, our soul necessarily receives the reasons of forms, in the same manner as a mirror the images of things. But from hence she imparts them through nature to matter, and to these material bodies: for we are certain that Nature*

---

*Nature is that divisible life which subsists about body, which is productive of seeds, and which is the cause to all bodies of vegetation, nutrition, and increase: but this life is void of phantasy, as is evident from its being distributed through every part of the body, and becoming by this means passive in the most eminent degree, whereas the phantasy, which is the summit of the irrational life, is undistributed and impassive.

is the artificer of bodies, as a whole of the universe; but as subsisting in individuals, of every thing which has the relation of a part. But nature in energy subsists in us without phantasy; and soul above this is endued with phantasy. If therefore it be confessed that nature contains the cause of things of which she possesses no phantasy, what by the gods should hinder us from assigning this prerogative to soul, by a much better and more ancient right; since we know this very particular in a phantastic manner, and at the same time apprehend it by a reasoning energy? Besides, where is the person so contentious, who will allow that material reasons subsist in nature, all indeed in capacity, though not all according to the same in energy, and yet will not allow this to soul? If, therefore, forms subsist in nature in capacity, and not in energy*, and likewise subsist in soul, but more pure and distinct, so as that they can be apprehended and known, but yet are by no means in energy; from whence do we derive the firm persuasion of the perpetuity of generation? Or where can our intellect find any

---

*Forms subsist in Nature fabricative, but not intellective; in partial souls like ours, intellective but not fabricative; and in divine souls and intellects, both fabricative and intellective.

stability in arguments respecting the eternity of the world? For a circular body is a composite of subject and form. It is necessary therefore, that though these are not separate from each other in energy, yet in our conceptions we should consider forms as having a prior and more ancient subsistence.

Since therefore it is admitted, that a certain preceding cause of material forms, in itself perfectly immaterial, is in subjection to the third artificer of things, who is not only the father and lord of these, but also of the apparent and fifth body; hence, separating Attis from this deity, as a cause descending as far as to matter, we are persuaded that Attis or Gallus is a prolific god. But, according to the fable, this god being placed near the whirling streams of the river Gallus, obtained a flourishing condition of being, and afterwards appearing beautiful and grand, was beloved by the mother of the gods; who, after she had committed all things to his charge, placed on his head a starry hat. But since this apparent heaven thus covers the head of Attis, is it proper to interpret the river Gallus as signifying the Gallaxy? For here a passive body is said to be mingled with the impassive circulation of the fifth body. And thus far the mother of the gods permitted this beautiful and intellectual god Attis, who is similar to the solar rays, to leap and dance. But when, in the course of his progression, he arrived at the extremity of things, the fable relates that he came into a cavern, and had connection with a nymph, obscurely signifying by this, the humid nature of matter*; though indeed matter is not so much signified here, as that last incorporeal cause which presides over matter; for, according to Heraclitus,

"Death is the portion of the humid soul."

Such, then, is the intellectual god Gallus, *i.e.* a deity who contains in himself material and sublunary forms, and who associates with the cause presiding over the fluctuating nature of matter. But he does not associate with the nymph as one with another of the same dignity and rank, but after the manner of one falling into matter. Who then is the mother of the gods? She is indeed the fountain of the intellectual and demiurgic gods who govern the apparent series of things: or

---

*See more concerning this in my translation of Porphyry's Cave of the Nymphs.

eertainly a deity producing things, and at the
same time subsisting with the mighty Jupiter; a goddess mighty, after one mighty, and
conjoined with the mighty demiurgus of the
world. She is the mistress of all life, and
the cause of all generation, who most easily
confers perfection on her productions, and
generates and fabricates things without passion, in conjunction with the father of the
universe. She is also a virgin, without a
mother, the assessor of Jupiter, and the true
parent of all the gods: for receiving in herself the causes of all the intelligible supermundane gods, she becomes a fountain to the
intellectual gods. The mother of the gods
therefore, subsisting after this manner, and
who is also called *Providence,* was inflamed
with an impassive love of Attis: for she vol-
untarily comprehends not only material
forms, but much more the causes of these.
But, according to the fable, this divine
providence, which preserves all generaated
and perishable natures, fell in love with
their demiurgic and prolific cause, and exhorted him to generate rather in an intelligible nature, and to be willing to convert
himself to her essence, and to dwell with her

divinity; and lastly, she commanded him to associate with no other than herself.

But her intention in these injunctions was, that he might at the same time pursue a salutary union, and avoid verging to matter. Hence she ordered him to behold her, as she was the fountain of the demiurgic gods, and this without being drawn downwards or allured into generation. For by this means the mighty Attis would become an artificer in a more excellent degree; since in all things conversion to a better nature is more efficacious than a propensity to a worse condition of being. For the fifth body, indeed, is on this account more fabricative and divine than terrestrial natures, because it is more converted to the gods. But no one will dare to affirm that a body, though it should be composed of the purest æther, is better than an undefiled soul, such as the demiurgus assigned to Hercules: for his soul, prior to her incarnation, then was, and appeared to be, more efficacious than when she consented to a conjunction with body. For a providential attention to these inferior concerns is much easier to Hercules now, having wholly departed to his universal father*, than it was formerly,

---

*Let the reader carefully remember that Hercules is

when, being invested with flesh, he was edu-
cated among men. So much more efficacious
to every nature is a conversion to that which
is better, than an apostization to that which
is worse. But the fable, desirous to signify
this, says, that the mother of the gods exhorted Attis to take care of himself, and
neither depart any where else, nor be capti-
vated with any other: but Attis, departing
from the mother of the gods, descended even
to the very extremity of matter. Hence, since
it was necessary that infinity should, some
time or other, be restrained and stop in its
progression, Corybas, or the mighty sun,
who has the same establishment as the
mother of the gods, who fabricated, and
providentially governs, all things in conjunction with her, and who performs nothing
without her, persuaded the lion to announce
the descent of Attis into the lowest matter.
Who then is the lion? We are told for a cer-
tainty that he was yellow: he is therefore a
cause presiding over a hot and fiery nature;
which cause was hereafter to contend with a

___

said to have been the son of Jupiter, because, during his
subsistence on the earth, he immutably preserved a commanding or ruling life, over which Jupiter presides, and
knew that he descended from Jupiter: and a similar reasoning must be preserved in the characters of the other
heroes.

nymph and emulate her association with Attis.

But who the nymph is, we have already explained: and the lion is said to be subservient to the demiurgic providence of things, *i.e.* without doubt, to the mother of the gods; and afterwards by his detecting and betraying Attis, to have been the cause of his castration. But castration* is a certain repression of infinity: for things in generation are not established in bounded forms, and restrained by a demiurgic providence, without that which is called the insanity of Attis; which, when it departs from measure, and transcends all bound, becomes, as it were, debilitated, and is no longer able to preserve the prerogative of its nature. And it is not irrational to believe that this should take place about the last cause among the gods. Behold, therefore, the fifth body unaltered according to every variation, and terminated by the illuminations of the moon, that this rising and perishing world may be in the vicinity of the fifth body. For, in the illuminations of the moon, we perceive that a certain variation and passion takes place. It is by no means

---

*Castration among the gods signifies the prolific progression of secondary divine causes into a subject order.

therefore absurd to assert, that Attis is a certain demigod, (for this is the meaning of the fable) or rather he is in reality a god: for he proceeds from the third demiurgus, and after his castration is again recalled to the mother of the gods; but as he persuaded himself wholly to verge, he appears to incline* into matter. Indeed he who considers this deity as the last of the gods, but the head of all the divine genera, will by no means deviate from the truth; for on this account the fable calls him a demigod†, that it may evince the difference between him and the im-

---

*It must ever be remembered that the gods comprehend and preside over the whole of things in an impassive and immaterial manner.

†As Attis is the artificer of things conversant with generation and corruption, he may be called a dæmon with respect to a god who is the artificer of immutable natures: not that he is a dæmon *essentially,* but only according to *analogy;* for as it is the employment of essential dæmons to attend on the gods and proximately preside over inferior natures; so each subordinate order of gods, from following the operations of its proximate superior order, and presiding over subject natures, may be called analogically, dæmoniacal with respect to that order. It is in this sense of the word that Plato, in the Timæus, calls the sublunary gods *dæmons* in one place, and in another *gods of gods;* and that in the Banquet he calls *Love a mighty dæmon,* and in the Phædrus a *god.* I only add, that the superficial writers on mythology of the present day, from being ignorant of this particular, have dogmatically asserted that Plato only believed in one god, and that he considered all the other powers subordinate to this god, as nothing more than dæmons; but nothing can be more false than such an assertion; for in the

mutable gods. And the Corybantes*, who
are the three ruling hypostases of the more
excellent genera after the gods, were placed
round him by the mother of the gods as his
guards.

But Attis likewise rules over the lions,
who, being allotted a hot and fiery nature, together with the lion, their leader, are indeed,
in the first place, the causes of safety to fire;
and through the heat and motive energy derived from thence, preserve other natures
from decay. Add too, that Attis spreads
himself round the heavens, which cover him
like a tiara, and tends, as it were, from
thence to the earth. And after this manner
does the mighty Attis present himself to our
view; and from hence the lamentations for
his long departure, and concealment, for his
vanishings and falling into a cavern, arise.
But the time in which his mysteries are performed sufficiently evinces the truth of what
I have here advanced: for they say that the
sacred tree should be cut down on the very

speech of Diotima in the Banquet, Plato clearly places
the genus of *dæmons* as a medium between *gods* and
men.

---

*The *Corybantes* form the unpolluted, guardian triad of
the *supermundane* order of gods, and are analogous to
the *Curetes* in the *intellectual* order.

day when the sun arrives at the extremity of the equinoctial arch; that on the following day the sounding of the trumpets should take place; that on the third day the sacred and arcane fertile crop of the god Gallus should be cut down; and that after all this, the hilaria and festive days should succeed.

That this excision therefore, which is so celebrated by many, is nothing more than a repression of infinity, is evident from this ceremony commencing when the mighty sun has arrived at the *equinoctial* circle, in which place his course receives the greatest circumscription: for that which is *equal* is bounded, but the *unequal* is infinite and incapable of being passed over. At this period, therefore, the section of the tree takes place; and after this the remaining ceremonies follow; some of them indeed, through mystic and secret institutions, but others, according to rites which may be divulged to all men. But by the section of the tree, the gods, in my opinion, symbolically teach us that, plucking the most beautiful of productions from the earth, it is necessary to offer virtue in conjunction with piety to the goddess, as a symbol of having lived in a becoming manner in the pres-

M

ent state. For a tree indeed germinates from the earth, but hastens, as it were, to shoot up into æther; it is likewise beautiful to behold, affords a cool shade in the heats of summer, sends forth fruits from itself, and liberally bestows them on mankind, through the abundant fertility which it possesses. The sacred institution, therefore, exhorts us, who are naturally celestial plants, though detained on the earth, that collecting together virtue in conjunction with piety from a terrestrial polity, we should eagerly hasten to the primogenial and vivific mother of the gods. But the recalling signal by the sound of a trumpet, which is given to Attis immediately after his castration, is also a signal to us, who, flying from heaven, have fallen upon earth. But after this symbol king Attis stops his infinity through the castration; and the gods by this means exhort us also to cut off the infinity of our nature, and hasten back again to that which is bounded and uniform, and, if possible, to *the one itself;* after which, when perfectly accomplished, it is proper that the *hilaria* should succeed. For what can be more joyful, what can be the occasion of greater hilarity, than the soul flying from infinity and generation, and the storms in which it is perpetually involved, and by this means returning to the gods themselves? But Attis being among the number of these, the mother of the gods by no means neglected him in his progressions beyond what was proper, but commanding him to restrain his infinity, converted him to herself.

But let not any one suspect that all this is said as of things which were once performed or really existed; as if the gods were ignorant what they should fabricate, or had any concerns which it was proper they should correct. For the ancients in interpreting the causes of things which have a perpetual subsistence, or rather in exploring the nature of the gods under the inspiring influence of the gods themselves, when they had discovered the objects of their investigation, concealed them under the veil of incredible fables*, that through the paradoxical and apparently incongruous nature of the fictions, we might be secretly excited to an enquiry after the truth; an utility which is merely irrational, and which takes place through symbols only, being, in my opinion, sufficient for

---

*See more concerning this in my translation of Sallust on the Gods and the World.

the simple part of mankind; but to those who are prudentially skilful, an emolument respecting the truth of the gods can then alone take place, when any one inquiring after it, discovers and receives it under the guiding influence of the gods themselves. And such a one, indeed, will be admonished by the ænigmas, that it is necessary to investigate something concerning them; and when he has discovered their signification, will advance through contemplation to the end, and, as it were, summit of the concealed truth; and this not through reverence and faith of a foreign opinion, rather than by the exercise of another energy, which subsists alone according to intellect.

In short, whatever we conceive having a subsistence as far as to the fifth body, I do not mean that which is intelligible only, but likewise these apparent bodies*, which are of an impassive and divine condition, as far as to these, the *pure*† gods are understood to sub-

---

i.e. The celestial bodies.

†The celestial gods may be called *pure* with respect to the sublunary gods from the bodies which are their participants; *i.e.* because a celestial is so much purer than a sublunary body. For as the essences of all the gods are transcendently pure, when one deity is called purer than another, this can only be understood as implying that the participant suspended from the one is purer than that of the other.

sist: but matter eternally proceeded, together with the prolific essence of the gods by whom these inferior natures were produced. And that providence of things, which is eternally consubsistent with the gods, through the superplenal abundance of prolific and demiurgic cause which they possess, and which being seated together with king Jupiter, is the fountain of the intellectual gods;—this divine providence adorns, rectifies, and transfers to a better state, that which is apparently void of life, unprolific, abject, and, as it may be said, the very dregs and sediment of things; and this it accomplishes through that which is last in the gods, and in which all their essences end. For Attis having a tiara ornamented with stars, evidently implies that he establishes, as the beginning of his government, the visible allotments of all the gods in this apparent world. But whatever is sincere and pure in the universe extends as far as to the galaxy: and, as about this place, that which is passive is mingled with the impassive, and matter subsists together with such a mixture; hence a communication with matter is the descent of Attis into a cavern, which, though it did not take place contrary to the will of the gods, and to the mother of the gods, yet it is said to have been contrary to their desire; for the gods naturally subsisting in that which is more excellent, that better condition of being, is by no means willing that they should be drawn down to these degraded concerns; but through the accommodating descent of more excellent beings, these lowest natures also are led back to a mode of subsistence more excellent and more friendly to divinity. Hence the mother of the gods is said not to have pursued Attis with hatred after his castration, but then to have been indignant no longer; but she is said to have been indignant on account of his descent, because, though of a more excellent condition, and a god, yet he gave himself up to an inferior nature. But the goddess repressing the progression of his infinity, and adorning that which was unadorned, through sympathy with the equinoctial circle, where the mighty sun governs the most perfect measure of bounded motion, willingly recalled the god to herself, or rather she retains him perpetually with herself; nor did these particulars ever subsist otherwise than at present, but *Attis is always the minister and charioteer of the mother of the gods*, and always desires the realms of generation; and lastly, always cuts off infinity through the bounded cause of forms.

Again, when Attis was led back, as it were, from the earth, he is said to have recovered the possession of his ancient sceptres; not that in reality he ever fell from them, or ever will; but he is said to have deserted his dominion, on account of his being mingled with a passive nature*. But it is perhaps worth investigating why, since the equinoctial is twofold, we do not celebrate the mysteries of this god when the sun is in Libra, but when he is in Aries; the reason therefore of this is beyond all doubt obvious: for when the sun first approaches to us, then advancing from the equinoctial, and the days increasing, this season, in my opinion, appeared the most convenient of all others for the occasion. And indeed, without having recourse to the reason, which asserts that light is the domestic associate of the gods, I can readily believe that the reductorial rays of the sun are aptly accommodated to those who hasten to be liberated from the realms of generation.

But consider this affair clearly as follows:

---

*i.e. From his presiding over a passive nature.

the sun draws all things from the earth, and calls them upwards with a resuscitating and wonderful heat; separating bodies, as it appears to me, as far as to the most exquisite subtilty, and elevating things which are naturally borne downwards. But all such effects as these are arguments of his unapparent powers: for how is it possible that he, who through corporeal heat can produce such effects in bodies, should not much more draw upwards and lead back again fortunate souls, through an unapparent, perfectly incorporeal, divine, and pure essence established in his rays? Hence, since it appears that this light is allied to the gods, and to such as hasten to return from whence they fell, and a light of this kind is increased in our world, so that the day is longer than the night, when the royal sun begins to proceed through the ram;—hence, the naturally reductorial power of the rays of the god is shewn by his apparent and unapparent energy, through which a great multitude of souls are led back again, by following the most splendid and eminently solar form of the senses: for the sense of sight is celebrated by the divine Plato* as not only lovely and useful for the purposes of life, but

*In the Timæus.

as a leader in the acquisition of wisdom. But if I should touch upon that arcane and mystic narration which the Chaldean†, agitated by divine fury, poured forth about the *seven-rayed god,* and through which he leads souls back again to the courts of light, I should speak of things unknown, and indeed vehemently so, to the sordid vulgar, though well known to theurgic and blessed men; and therefore I shall be silent respecting such particulars at present.

But, as I before observed, the time appointed by the antients for the celebration of these sacred rites was not irrationally assumed, but with the greatest propriety, and agreeable to the most perfect reason: and an argument for the truth of this may be derived from considering, that the venerable and arcane mysteries of Ceres and Proserpine* are celebrated when the sun is in Libra; and this with the greatest propriety; for it is necessary to be again initiated when the solar god is departing from our zone, that we may suffer no molestation from the prevalence of

---

†*i.e.* Julian the Theurgist.
*See my Dissertation on the Eleusinian and Bacchic Mysteries.

an atheistical and dark power.   Hence the
Athenians celebrate the mysteries of Ceres
twice; the lesser mysteries when the sun is in
Aries, and the greater when he is in Libra;
through the causes which I have already assigned.   But it appears to me that they were
called *greater* and *lesser* on other accounts,
but especially for this reason, because it is
more proper to celebrate these mysteries
when the god is departing from, than when
he is approaching to, our zone.   Hence, in
the lesser mysteries, the *proteleia** of initiation take place, and this so far only as is sufficient for the purposes of recollection; as the
saving and reductorial god is at this period
present.   But a little after this, continued
lustrations, and the performance of holy
ceremonies belonging to the sacred mysteries, succeed: but when the god departs from
us to the region of the Antichthones, then the
very summit of the mysteries receives its
consummation.   But see how, as in the mysteries of Gallus, the cause of generation is
cut off, so among the Athenians, those who

---

*The mysteries consisted of three parts τελετη, μυησις,
εποπτεια, *i.e. certain perfective rites, initiation,* and *inspection;* and the *proteleia,* or *things previous to perfection,* belonged to the two first of these parts, but not to the
third.

are concerned in the arcana are perfectly holy; and the hierophant who presides over these entirely abstains from all generation, as one to whom a progression into the infinitive by no means belongs, but an essence bounded, and perpetually abiding, contained in one, undecaying and pure. And thus much may suffice respecting particulars of this kind.

It now remains that we investigate the sanctity and lustrations belonging to the mysteries of Gallus and the Mother of the Gods, that if we should find any thing in these pertaining to our hypothesis we may transfer it from thence. But this, in the first place, appears ridiculous to every one, that the sacred law permits in these mysteries the feeding on flesh, but prohibits the use of vegetables; for are not the latter deprived of, but the former endued with, soul? And is not flesh full of blood and many other things which both the sight and the hearing cannot easily endure? Is not this too the greatest argument in favour of vegetables, that injury to no one results from their use; but no one can feed on flesh without the slaughter of animals, the execution of which must necessarily be at-

tended with affliction and pain? Such are
the objections which may be raised by many,
and those not of the vulgar of mankind: and
these very particulars are now derided by the
most impious*; for, say they, in these rites,
the stalks of pot-herbs may be eaten, but the
roots must be rejected, as likewise turnips;
and again, figs are allowed, but pomegran-
ates and apples are not permitted to be
eaten. As I have often heard many murmur-
ing about particulars of this kind, and have
myself formerly started the same objections,
I alone among all men seem to owe the
tribute of thanks to all the gods, but especially to the mother of the gods, not only on
account of her beneficence towards me in
other affairs, but for her goodness in not
neglecting me as one wandering in darkness;
but, in the first place, commanding me to cut
off, not indeed from my body, but from the
irrational impulses and motions of my soul,
whatever is considered as superfluous and
vain by the intellectual and presiding cause
of our souls; and in the next place, establish-
ing in my intellect certain reasons, which are
perhaps not perfectly abhorrent from the

*Meaning the Christians, Epicureans, and *perfect*
Atheists.

true and holy science concerning the gods.—
But my discourse seems to revolve in a circle,
as if I had nothing to say on this occasion;
this, however, is far from being the case; for
in running through the several particulars, I
am able to exhibit clear and manifest causes
why it is not lawful to feed on those vegetables which the sacred institution prohibits,
and this I shall very shortly accomplish; but
at present it is better to propose, as it were,
certain formula and rules, by following which
we may be able to form a judgement of any
particulars which, through the haste of com-
position, may have escaped our attention:
and, in the first place, it is necessary briefly
to call to mind the account which we have
given of Attis and his castration, and the
meaning of the symbols which take place
after his castration as far as to the hilaria,
together with the intention of the sacred lustrations. Attis, then, has been said by us to
be a certain cause and divinity who proximately fabricates the material world, and
who, descending even to the extremity of
things, is at length stopt by the demiurgic
motion of the sun, when the solar god arrives
at the extreme bounded circumference of the
universe, and which, from its effect, is called

the equinoctial circle. But we have said that castration is the restraining of infinity, which takes place no otherwise than by a revocation and emersion to a more antient and primary cause; but we consider the elevation of souls as the ultimate design of lustration.

These sacred rites, therefore, do not permit us, in the first place, to feed on seeds which decline towards the earth: for earth is the last of things, into which evil, according to Plato, being impelled, perpetually revolves; and the gods in the Oracles every where denominate it dregs, and continually exhort us to fly from thence. In the first place, therefore, the vivific and providential goddess does not permit us to use aliment which declines towards the earth, but exhorts us to look to heaven, or rather above the heavens themselves. There are some, indeed, who feed on one kind of seed only, that is, on beans, which they consider as not ranking among seeds any more than pot-herbs, since they naturally rise upwards and are straight, and do not drive their roots in the earth, but are rooted in the same manner as the fruit of the ivy depends from the tree, or that of the vine from the reed: on this account therefore, the goddess forbids us to use the seed of plants, but permits us to feed on fruits and pot-herbs; not indeed on such as are almost level with the ground, but on such as are sublimely raised from the earth. In like manner, with respect to turnips, she orders us to abstain from whatever they possess of a terrestrial nature, merely on account of its alliance to earth; but she allows us the use of whatever emerges upwards and raises itself on high, on account of the purity of its nature. Hence, she permits us to use the stalks of pot-herbs, but forbids us to feed on the roots, and especially from such as are nourished in, and sympathize with, the earth.

Again, with respect to the fruits of trees, she prohibits us from corrupting and consuming apples, as being sacred and golden, and images of the rewards attending arcane and telestic labours*; and as deserving reverence and respect, on account of their exemplars: but she forbids the use of the pomegranate as being a terrestrial plant; and likewise the fruit of the palm, because, perhaps some one may say, it does not grow in Phrygia, where this sacred institution was first es-

---

*He alludes to the Hesperian golden apples which were plucked by Hercules, which formed his last labour, and signify his reaping undefiled advantages through mystic operations; for gold is a symbol of purity.

tablished: but to me, the prohibition seems
rather to arise from its being a plant sacred
to the sun, and of an undecaying nature, and
that on this account it is not assumed in the
purifying rites for the nourishment of the
body. But after this, we are forbidden to
feed on any kind of fish, the reason of which
is, a problem in common with us and the
Egyptians. But it appears to me, that any
one may, with great propriety, always abstain from fish, for two reasons, and especially in purifying ceremonies: In the first
place, because it is not proper to feed on
things which we sacrifice to the gods; and
here, indeed, I shall have no occasion to fear
being accused of gluttony, which I recollect
was once the case, should any one enquire why
we do not frequently sacrifice these to the
gods; for we have something to offer in reply
to this interrogation. And we sacrifice these,
indeed, O blessed man, in certain telestic
rites; just as the Romans sacrifice a horse,
and, both Greeks and Romans, many other
animals and wild beasts, as, for instance,
dogs to Hecate: and among other nations, in
telestic sacrifices, such like victims are of-
fered, once or twice a year. But this is not
the case in the most honoured sacrifices,

through which alone we are rendered worthy of entering into communion and banqueting with the gods. Hence, we do not sacrifice fishes in the most venerable rites, because we neither feed on them, nor take any care of their propagation; nor, lastly, have we any herds of fishes, as we have of oxen and sheep; for as these animals are assisted and multiplied through the attention which we pay to them, they are on this account useful to us for other purposes, and for honourable sacrifices to the gods : and this is one reason why I do not think it is proper to feed on fish during the time of the purifying rites.

But the other reason, and which, I think, harmonizes better with what has been before said, is this, that fishes being after a certain manner merged in the profundities of the earth, are more terrestrial than seeds; but he who desires to fly away, and soar sublimely above the air to the very summit of the heavens, will justly abhor every thing of this kind, and will pursue and convert himself to natures tending towards the air, and hastening to arduous sublimities, and, that I may speak in poetical language, beholding the heavens. Again, this sacred institution permits us to feed on birds, a few excepted, which happen to be perfectly sacred; and likewise all quadrupeds which we usually feed on, except the hog: for as this animal is entirely terrestrial in its form, manner of living, and from the very condition of its essence, (as its flesh is excrementitious and gross*) on this account it is driven from the sacred feast: for this victim is not undeservedly considered as friendly to the terrestrial gods; since it is an animal which never beholds the heavens, and is not only unwilling, but is naturally incapable of such a survey.

And such are the causes why the divine institution says that it is proper to abstain from certain species of aliment, and which we ourselves understanding, communicate to those who possess a knowledge of the gods. We shall only therefore observe, concerning other particulars, the use of which is permitted, that the sacred institution does not prescribe all things to all; but the divine law, regarding that which is possible to human nature, permits the multitude to use common aliment of this kind; not that we should all

---

*I have observed that the most vulgar and gross part of mankind are remarkably fond of pork; and this very properly, since like rejoices in like.

of us necessarily equally abstain in all things, (for this perhaps is not easy to be accomplished) but that we should, in the first place, feed on that aliment which the power of the body will readily admit; which, in the second place, we possess the ability of obtaining; and thirdly, to which our will assents. For in sacred rites it is well worth extending the will in such a manner that it may rise above the power of body, and may cheerfully endeavour to comply with the divine institutions; for this, indeed, is eminently conducive to the safety of the soul—to pay a much greater attention to itself, than to the salubrity of the body; and even the body, though in a secret manner, will appear to receive by this means greater and more wonderful advantages: for when the soul gives the whole of herself to the gods, and wholly delivers herself to the guidance of better natures, purifying rites, as it appears to me, succeeding, and prior to these, divine institutions taking the lead, nothing farther now prohibiting and impeding; for all things are contained in the gods, and subsist about them) when this is the case, the divine light will immediately shine upon her. But in consequence

of her being thus deified, she transfuses a
certain vigorous strength into her connate
spirit, which, when included, and, as it were,
possessing dominion, becomes through this
spirit the cause of safety to the whole body.
For that all diseases, or at least the greater
part, and the greatest, happen from the mu-
tation and erroneous motion of the spirit,
will not, I think, be denied by any physician:
for, according to some, all diseases, and according to others, the greater part, and the
greatest, and the most difficult to be cured,
originate from hence. And indeed the Oracles
of the gods testify the truth of these assertions, when they declare, that through purifying ceremonies, not the soul only, but
bodies themselves, become worthy of receiving much assistance and health: "for (say
they) the mortal vestment of bitter matter
will, by this means, be preserved*." And
this the gods in an exhortatory manner, announce to the most holy of Theurgists.

---

*This is most probably one of the Chaldæan Oracles,
but is not to be found among the fragments of the Zoro-
astrian Oracles, collected first by Patricius, and afterwards republished by Stanley. Among these fragments,
however, the following Oracle is to be found, which perfectly corresponds in meaning with that quoted by our
pious Emperor:

Εκτεινας πυρινον νουν
Εργον επ’ ευσεβιης, ρευστον και σωμα σαωσεις.

What therefore now remains for us to say; especially since we have composed this Oration without any respite in a short part of one night, without any previous reading or meditation on the subject, and without even intending to discourse on these particulars, till we called for these note books in order to commit them to writing? The goddess herself is a witness of the truth of my assertion. What then remains for us to accomplish, except recalling the goddess into our memory, together with Minerva and Bacchus, whose festivals the law establishes in these purifying rites? And this indeed took place, in consequence of the authors of these ceremonies perceiving the alliance of Minerva with the mother of the gods, through providential similitude in the essence of each; from perceiving likewise the partial fabrication of Bacchus, which this mighty god receiving from the uniform and stable life of the mighty Jupiter, in consequence of proceeding from him, distributed to all apparent natures; at the same time administring and ruling over every partial fabrication. But it

i.e. "By extending a fiery intellect to the work "of piety, you will preserve the flowing body." But the Oracle by a fiery intellect, means an intellect full of divine conceptions, and which profoundly beholds the nature of the gods.

is proper likewise to call to mind, in conjunction with these, Hermes *Epaphroditus**; for
thus is this god denominated by the mystics,
who are said to kindle lamps in honour of
the wise Attis. Who, therefore, is so dull of
apprehension as not to understand that all
things which entirely subsist for the sake of
generation are called upward thorugh Hermes and Venus†? And this recalling power
is especially the characteristic of reason; but
is not Attis he, who, a little before being im-
prudent, is now, through his castration, denominated wise? For he was before unwise,
because he connected himself with matter, and
undertook the government of generation: but
he is now wise, because he has adorned with
beauty the sordid nature of matter, and has
so vanquished its deformity, as to surpass
all the imitative art and intelligence of man.

---

*That is, *beautiful,* or *graceful,* a name which was
doubtless given to Hermes from his intimate alliance with
Venus; for Mercury forms the summit of the *harmonic*
and *elevating,* or *reductorial* supermundane triad, which
consists of *Mercury, Venus, Apollo.* To which we may
add, that the Greek word επαφρος, Epaphros, signifies *one upon whom there is foam;* and foam implies, as
Proclus on the Cratylus beautifully observes in his account of Venus, *purity of nature, prolific light and power,
and, as it were, the highest flower of life.*

†And this because they belong to the supermundane
reductorial triad, which elevates through *Truth, Beauty,
and Harmony.*

But what will be the end of this discourse?
Is it not evident that it should close with a
hymn to the mighty goddess?

A mother of gods and men! O assistant
and partner in the throne of mighty Jupiter!
O fountain of the intellectual gods! O thou
whose nature concurs with the uncontami-
nated essences of intelligibles, and who, receiving a common cause from all intelligibles,
dost impart it to intellectual natures! Vivific
goddess, Counsel and Providence, and the
fabricator of our souls! O thou who didst
love the mighty Bacchus, who didst preserve
the castrated Attis, and when he had fallen
into the cavern of earth, didst again lead him
upwards to his pristine abode! O thou who
art the leader of every good to the intellectual gods, with which thou dost likewise fill
this sensible world, and who dost impart to
us all possible good in every thing belonging
to our nature! Graciously bestow upon all
men felicity, the summit of which is the
knowledge of the gods: but especially grant
to the Roman people in common, that they
may wipe away the stains of their impiety;
and that they may be blessed with prosperous fortune, which, in conjunction with them,
may govern the empire for many thousands

of years. But with respect to myself, may the fruit of my cultivation of thy divinity be the possession of truth in dogmata concerning the gods, perfection in Theurgy, in all the actions which I shall undertake, both political and military, virtue, in conjunction with good fortune; and lastly a departure from the present life without pain, and attended with glory, together with good hope of a progression to thy divinity.

To the

ANCIENT PLATONIC PHILOSOPHERS

✠

HAIL souls triumphant! Truth is all your own,
Lov'd by the wise, to Folly's sons unknown.
Let Ign'rance proudly boast her tyrant reign,
Her num'rous vot'ries, and her wide domain,
Your wisdom scorn, and with barbaric hand
Spread *dire delusion* thro' a falling land.
By you inspir'd, the glorious talk be mine,
To rise from Sense, and seek a life divine;
From Phantasy, the soul's Calypso, free,
To fail secure on Life's tempestuous sea,
Led by your doctrines like the Pleiads' light,
With guiding radiance streaming thro' the night,
From mighty Neptune's overwhelming ire,
Back to the palace of my lawful Sire.

THE END

www.ingramcontent.com/pod-product-compliance
Lightning Source LLC
LaVergne TN
LVHW061941060326
832903LV00047B/252